Vampires

Tony Lee

Badger Publishing Limited
Oldmedow Road,
Hardwick Industrial Estate,
King's Lynn PE30 4JJ
Telephone: 01438 791037

www.badgerlearning.co.uk

2 4 6 8 10 9 7 5 3

Vampires ISBN 978-1-78464-032-3

Text © Tony Lee 2014

Complete work © Badger Publishing Limited 2014

Publisher: Susan Ross
Senior Editor: Danny Pearson
Publishing Assistant: Claire Morgan
Designer: Fiona Grant
Series Consultant: Dee Reid

Photos: Cover Image: Getty/Ivan Bliznetsov
Page 5: © Vincenzo Dragani/Alamy
Page 6: © Zoonar GmbH/Alamy
Page 7: British Library/Robana/REX
Page 8: © Nature Picture Library/Alamy
Page 12: UIG via Getty Images
Page 13: Image Broker/REX
Page 16: © AF archive/Alamy
Page 18: Getty Images/Frederick M. Brown/Stringer
Page 19: ITV/REX
Page 20: © dpa picture alliance/Alamy
Page 24: © Moviestore collection Ltd/Alamy
Page 25: © AF archive/Alamy
Page 26: © Pictorial Press Ltd/Alamy
Page 27: © AF archive/Alamy
Page 28: © AF archive/Alamy
Page 29: © Photos 12/Alamy

Attempts to contact all copyright holders have been made.
If any omitted would care to contact Badger Learning, we will be happy to make appropriate arrangements.

Contents

Vocabulary

ancient	popular
betrayed	programme
character	reflection
impaled	supernatural

1. THE BEGINNINGS

The first stories about Dracula were written just over a hundred years ago, but the words 'vampire' and 'vampyre' have been around for centuries.

They were first used in Eastern Europe in stories about people who returned from the dead to drink the blood of the living.

In the 1800s there were many news stories in Europe of people who said that their relatives had died and returned as vampires.

People liked to scare each other with the idea of a blood-drinking vampire, and so the legend of the vampire began.

In 1819, John Polidori wrote a book called *The Vampyre* about a Vampire called Count Ruthden.

This spooky story became a bestseller. Everybody wanted to read about vampires.

A 'penny dreadful' was an ongoing magazine that only cost a penny. Stories would be printed in parts over a number of weeks. The most popular vampire story was 'Varney the Vampire'.

Bram Stoker's vampire

In 1896, Bram Stoker wrote a book called *Dracula* about Count Dracula, who fed on the blood of his victims.

The story takes place in a spooky castle in Transylvania, Victorian London and also in Whitby in Yorkshire.

At the end of the story, Dracula's throat is cut and then he is stabbed in the heart. He crumbles to dust.

Why did Bram Stoker write such a blood-thirsty book?

Perhaps it was because he was often sick as a child and had to spend many weeks in bed. His mum read him lots of stories about death and the supernatural.

WOW! facts

The title of the book was going to be *The Un-Dead* but Stoker changed it at the last minute!

2. THE 'REAL' DRACULA

Many people believe that Bram Stoker's Dracula was based on the real life of a man called Vlad Tepes.

Vlad Tepes lived in the 1400s and was also known as Vlad the Impaler.

Vlad had a very hard life as a young man and this might have been why he turned out to be so cruel when he grew up.

Links between Bram Stoker's book and Vlad the Impaler:

In the book

- Van Helsing tells a story of two brothers, where one betrays the other.
- Bram Stoker called his vampire Dracula.

In Vlad's life

- he was betrayed by his brother like in Van Helsing's story.
- Vlad was nicknamed Dracula because his father was known as Dracul, the Dragon, and Dracula meant Son of the Dragon!

Why was he called Vlad the Impaler?

He was called this because his favourite way of killing people was by driving a wooden stake into their stomachs.

Then the stakes were hammered into the ground.

The people were left to slowly die.

Stories tell of Vlad inviting 500 lords to a feast.

When the feast was over, Vlad's soldiers rushed in and impaled all 500 men.

Another time he invited all the poor people from the town to come to a feast.

After the feast, the doors were closed and the building was burned to the ground with everyone inside.

In the story, Dracula sucks blood out of the necks of his victims.

Did Vlad the Impaler drink blood?

There are rumours that he did, but no real proof. But he did eat his meals beside the bodies, so maybe blood dripped into his dinner! Ergh!

14

Vlad didn't just like impaling people.

Sometimes he used different methods to kill people:

- Skinning people
- Boiling them alive
- Cutting off arms or legs or noses

It is said that he killed almost 100,000 people.

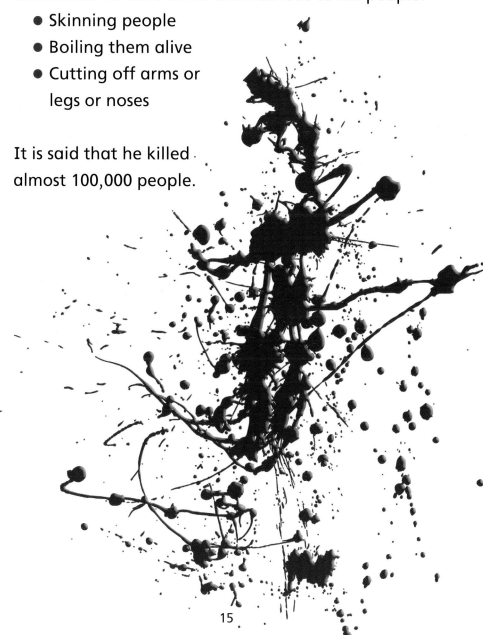

3. A WORLD OF VAMPIRES

There have been many famous vampires in books and films over the years – but where in the world are they from?

Here are some of the most well-known...

Europe:

Count Dracula *(Dracula)*

Count Orlok *(Nosferatu)*

Eli *(Let The Right One In)*

Mitchell *(Being Human)*

Lestat *(Interview with the Vampire)*

Vladimir Dracula *(Young Dracula)*

America:

Edward Cullen *(Twilight)*

Blade *(Blade)*

Louis *(Interview with the Vampire)*

Angel *(Buffy the Vampire Slayer)*

Count Von Count *(Sesame Street)*

Selene *(Underworld)*

David and his gang *(The Lost Boys)*

Ian *(The Vampire Diaries)*

Count von Count

Sometimes Dracula is not a scary figure.

In the children's programme Sesame Street, Count von Count looks like Dracula in the old films.

He wears a black cloak and has fangs for teeth.

But Count von Count is called the count because he loves to count things!

Count Duckula

In the 1990s, there was a cartoon called Count Duckula about a green duck who wore a cloak.

He lived in a castle with a torture chamber but he was not really evil and did not drink blood.

He liked to go around helping people!

4. HUNTING VAMPIRES

What signs should you look for when trying to spot a vampire?

- sharp fangs
- hates garlic
- hates sunlight
- no reflection in a mirror

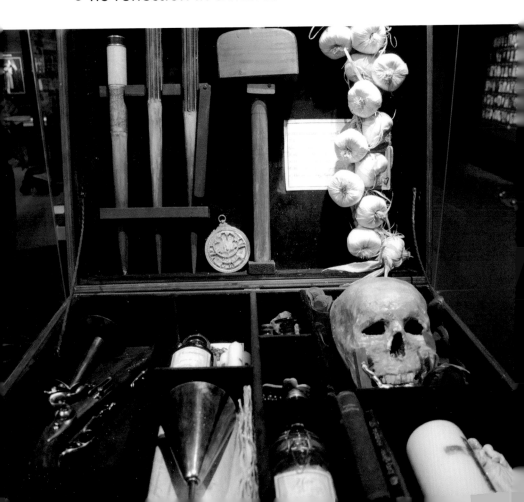

Ways to kill a vampire

Wooden stake: Ram this into the vampire's heart. Any sharp wood works.

Cut off the head: Use a sword or sharp knife to remove the head from the body.

Sunlight: WARNING! This doesn't work on some vampires. Dracula likes cloudy days. Edward Cullen just sparkles.

Ultraviolet light seems to work best.

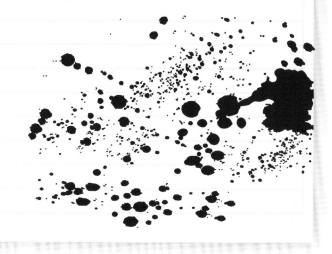

Garlic: If they eat or drink it, they explode. If it touches their skin, they burn. Held near them? They back away.

Cross: WARNING! A cross only makes a Vampire back away if you have faith in the cross.

If you don't believe, then don't bother.

Silver bullets: That won't work for some vampires (but it might stop a werewolf).

Fire: Setting them on fire is very risky as you might burn yourself!

DO NOT: Hug a vampire, kiss them, take them to the cinema, or fall in love with them.

5. VAMPIRES IN THE MEDIA

People like going to the cinema to be scared and there have been lots of films about scary vampires.

The black and white film *Nosferatu* was made in 1922.

Count Orlok in the film was one of the scariest vampires ever. He was also the first vampire to be killed by sunlight.

The film *Count Dracula* was first shown in 1931.
Dracula wore a cloak and had fangs for teeth.

These old films do not seem very scary to us now but
at the time people thought they were very scary.

WOW! facts

When *Count Dracula* was first
shown some people were so
scared they fainted!

A hundred and seventy films later, Dracula was still wearing a black cloak and had fangs for teeth, but the character of Dracula had changed.

Over the years he turned from a monster into the romantic lead.

The 1992 film *Dracula* was more of a love story than a horror story!

In the 1980s, vampires started to become cool.

In an early Lestat film, *Interview with the Vampire*, Lestat (played by Tom Cruise) is really evil, but in a later film, *Queen of the Damned*, he is very popular and even becomes a rock star!

In the film *The Lost Boys* the vampires are a street gang, with trendy clothes, good looks and dangerous habits.

In the TV show *Buffy the Vampire Slayer*, Angel, the vampire, is very good-looking and Buffy's true love.

Buffy does kill some vampires with a wooden stake, but most of the show is about her love for Angel.

The *Twilight* films about vampires are really love films.

In the films, Edward Cullen is a very good-looking vampire who drinks animal blood over human blood. He falls in love with a beautiful girl called Bella.

In these films many vampires are good guys!

Why have stories of creatures who kill people and drink their blood been so popular?

- People like to be scared.
- An evil character who drinks blood is about as scary as it gets.
- It's even better if that character can't be killed easily!

Questions

What year did John Polidori write his book *The Vampyre*? *(page 7)*

Who wrote *Dracula*? *(page 8)*

How many people did Vlad the Impaler kill? *(page 15)*

How can you spot a vampire? *(page 20)*

What year was the film *Nosferatu* made? *(page 24)*

What is the name of Buffy the Vampire Slayer's true love? *(page 28)*

INDEX